Old YARROW and ETTRICK

by
Alex F. Young

A baker's van emerging from Philiphaugh Estate at Ivy Lodge Gate in the early twentieth century. The lodge house was home to Mrs Ann Wilson of Channelkirk, a widow in her late sixties, and her two sons who worked on the estate. Thomas, born at Dirleton in 1846, was a garden labourer, and William, born in 1849 at Tranent, was a forester.

FURTHER READING

Angus, William: *Ettrick & Yarrow – A Guide*, pub. John
 Lewis, Selkirk, 1894.
Mackay, John James: *Border Highways*, pub. John James
 Mackay, 1998.
*Slater's Royal National Commercial Directory and Topography of
 Scotland*, pub. Isaac Slater, Manchester & London, 1867.
The County of Selkirk, Royal Commission of Ancient
 Monuments, HMSO, Edinburgh, 1957.
*The Topographical, Statistical and Historical Gazetteer of
 Scotland*, pub. A Fullarton & Co., London & Dublin,
 1847.
*An Inventory of Gardens and Designed Landscapes in Scotland,
 Vol. 5: Lothians & Borders*. A Report by Land Use
 Consultants to the Countryside Commission for
 Scotland, 1988.
The Statistical Account of Scotland, [Yarrow, Vol. 7 (1793) and
 Ettrick, Vol. 3 (1792)], pub. William Creech, Edinburgh.
The New Statistical Account of Scotland, Vol. 3, Roxburgh,
 Peebles and Selkirk, pub Wm. Blackwood & Sons,
 Edinburgh & London, 1845.
*The Third Statistical Account of Scotland; The Counties of
 Peebles & Selkirk*, pub. Collins, Glasgow, 1964.

ACKNOWLEDGEMENTS

The author wishes to thank Valerie Barrie, Jill Brown, Ann D.
Brunton, Walter and Ann Coltherd, Helen Currie, Jack
Davidson, Beth and Bill Gollan, Annie Hepburn, Sandra
Howat, Ivan and Carole Howden, James Irving, Daphne
Jackson, John and Nanette Marshall, Jimmy McVicar, Isabella
Shaw, the Rev. Samuel Siroky, Wendy and Gareth Whitehead,
Tommy and Mary Wilson, the Scottish Borders Archive and
Local History Centre, Selkirk, Stephen White of the Local
Studies Library, Carlisle, Ruth Airley of the Ewart Library,
Dumfries, Emma Rutherford of the Educational Institute of
Scotland, and the Scottish Youth Hostel Association, Stirling.

The publishers wish to thank the following for contributing
photographs to this book: Harry and Sheila Turnbull of
Ladhope for pages 18, 33 and 34, and Pauline Northam and
Elizabeth Reid of Ramsaycleuch for the inside back cover.

Philiphaugh House on a winter's afternoon around 1910. In 1528 Patrick Murray of
Falahill obtained a charter for the 2,799-acre Philiphaugh estate – later the site of the
1645 Battle of Philiphaugh in which the forces of the Royalist Marquis of Montrose
were routed by General David Leslie's Covenanters' army – but by 1842 the Murray
family was in such financial difficulties that the estate was sold to John Steel (1801–
1872) of the Hall of Cairnduff, Lanarkshire. In 1830 Steel married Grace (died 1880),
the daughter of James Strang of Westhouse, East Kilbride, and after this the family was
styled Strang Steel. In 1874 William Strang Steel (1832–1911), seen here in the car's
front passenger seat, had the 'large and picturesque white-harled Jacobean pile'
remodelled by the Edinburgh architect James Maitland Wardrop. In the early 1960s it
was demolished.

INTRODUCTION

Running their parallel courses through the hills towards Selkirk, the Yarrow and Ettrick valleys have their separate and distinct estates and communities. Scanning down each on Herman Moll's map of 1732 we find Bow, Newark Cast, Hangins, Duchore, Reskinhoop and Catslack on the Yarrow, while on the Ettrick there is Aikwood, Faldhoop, Dallerean, Tushyla, Thirlstain, Deepup and Etterickhouse.

Running into the Loch of the Lowes as the Yarrow Water, or the Little Yarrow, the River Yarrow flows into St Mary's Loch before meandering down the valley to join the Ettrick Water west of Selkirk. The Rev. Robert Russell attributes the derivation of the name to *Garw* in ancient British, *Garbh* in the Gaelic and *Garow* in the Cornish, meaning 'what is rough'. In the twelfth century charter of Selkirk Abbey, it was *Garua*, and later softened to *Zarof*, *Yharrow* and *Yara*.

Today's A-class road passes along the valley, connecting Moffat in Dumfriesshire with Selkirk, but it was not until 1887 that it carried a scheduled coach service. This road, in places, followed a different route in earlier times. On Roy's Military Map of 1750 it is shown on the south-east side of St Mary's Loch, crossing to the left bank by a ford near to Dryhope. Ainslie's map of 1773 shows a new route along the north west of the loch. Thomson's 1832 survey shows only the new route.

It is sometimes best to ignore the derivation of place names, or take the advice of the Rev. James Smith in the *New Statistical Account* and say that they are of doubtful origin; although he suggests that 'Ettrick' may have come from either the Gaelic, meaning furrow or trench, or from British aborigines to whom *Ed* signified a current and *Terig*, mud. The road along the Ettrick Valley from Selkirk may have carried the mail coach to Carlisle, through Eskdalemuir and hence to either Lockerbie or Langholm, but was always the poor relation to the Yarrow valley.

The area was once clothed by the Ettrick Forest – but the whole of Scotland was then, more or less, a forest. The disappearing woodland may have taken with it the wild deer, but in compensation its rich grassland supported sheep and, to a lesser extent, black cattle.

On the invitation of Mr William Strang Steel, members of the Western and Eastern sections of the Scottish Automobile Club met at Philiphaugh on Saturday, 23 July 1904. The party was entertained to luncheon and a tour of the house and grounds before assembling for this photograph. No known guest list survives but, judging from the registration marks, they were from Glasgow, Renfrew and Lanark in the west, and Edinburgh, Midlothian and Peebles in the east. The gentleman in the front car, Selkirkshire-registered LS 3, appears to be William Strang Steel. Today, the annual increase in the number of motor cars on our roads may be thought alarming but, according to Parliamentary returns of August 1904, Britain that year had 8,400 registered motor cars and 5,121 motorcycles on 1 January, numbers that had increased by 1 April the same year to 14,887 cars and 16,534 motorcycles.

The first *Statistical Account* (1793) records that Yarrow parish had 55,000 sheep and 545 black cattle, while Ettrick had 30,000 sheep and 230 head of cattle. Some forty years later the *New Statistical Account* reported that of the 70,000 acres in Yarrow's agricultural economy only 2,740 acres were in tillage – oats, 750 acres; barley, 250; hay, 500; turnip, 375; and potatoes, 125. Ettrick Parish extended to only 44,000 acres, divided among 29 farms, and due to its much narrower valley only 125 acres were under the plough. Ettrick, at that time, had 36 carts and 20 ploughs.

Until the close of the eighteenth century, Black Face sheep predominated in the flocks in the upper parts of valleys and although they thrived and produced good meat their wool was coarse, selling for only 6/- per stone, while in the sheltered lower areas what were thought to be less hardy breeds produced a finer wool fetching 18/- per stone. The early nineteenth century saw the introduction of Cheviots and Leicesters and an upturn in the agricultural economy, with the emphasis on wool. With improving roads, the transportation of the wool to Selkirk and its mills and railhead opened new markets.

But roads were not the only form of communication. In July 1893 the valleys were introduced to the telegraph – the first coming through Yarrow Post Office on 9 August: 'To Walter Beattie, Esq., Gordon Arms, Yarrow. Heartiest congratulations to the people of Yarrow on the inauguration of the telegraphic connection with the outside world. May Yarrow flourish. Paterson, Innerleithen.' The sentiment that Yarrow was now connected 'with the outside world' suggests, perhaps, that Innerleithen was then at the world's crossroads!

Today, farming remains a major factor in the valleys' economy, but there have been changes. Where once day trips in coaches and charabancs were run to St Mary's Loch from Selkirk and Innerleithen – and only the Gordon Arms, Tibbie Shiel's Inn, the Tushielaw Inn, and later the S.Y.H.A.'s hostels at Broadmeadows and Thirlestane offered overnight accommodation – there are now lodges, caravan parks and camping sites.

The conservatory at Philipshaugh in 1906. The origins of conservatories lie in the seventeenth century when they were used to 'conserve' ice, and the first all-glass conservatory was built at Syon Park Gardens, London, between 1827 and 1830. The idea caught on and, with the abolition of the Glass Tax in 1845, grew in popularity across the country, either as free standing structures in gardens or attached to a house with internal access. On the choice of the owner it could either be a general plant house, an orangery, a palm house, or a winter garden. It is not known when, or by whom, this one at Philiphaugh was built.

The General's Bridge at the East Lodge entrance to Bowhill Estate. A bridge appears at this entry to the estate on William Faden's map of 1807, but the bridge pictured, and the one at Faulshope, dates from 1834, following work on the house. The 'General' appears to have been Lieutenant-general Alexander Mackay, who leased the old house from the Scotts. Born in 1719, he was the son of George Mackay, 3rd Lord Reay. He received an ensign's commission in 1737 and in 1745 was a captain with Loudon's highlanders when he was taken prisoner at the Battle of Prestonpans on 21 September during which the Jacobites routed a government force under Sir John Cope; he escaped in December. In 1777 he was promoted to Lieutenant-general and appointed Commander in Chief of the army in Scotland in May 1780. His last service was as Governor of Stirling Castle in 1788, dying at Bowhill on 31 May 1789. On the Ettrick, the Weatherhouse entry to Bowhill crosses Colin's, or more correctly Cullen's, Bridge which is apparently named after a Major Cullen who had served with Mackay.

Under the shadow of Pernassie Hill, 'Sweet Bowhill' was originally a modest hunting lodge, built around 1708 by Lord Bowhill and acquired by the 2nd Duke of Buccleuch in 1747 to allow his son, Lord Charles Scott, to stand for parliament. The family, however, did not occupy the house, instead leasing it to, amongst others, Lieutenant-general Mackay. On his accession to the estate in 1812, the 4th Duke, Charles William Henry Montagu-Douglas, commissioned the architect William Atkinson (c.1773–1839) and the old house disappeared under a succession of additions and alterations. The work stopped in 1819, on the death of Charles, and was not resumed until 1831 when Walter Francis Montagu-Douglas-Scott (1806–1884), the 5th Duke, commissioned William Burn (1789–1870) of Edinburgh, and his nephew J. McVicar Anderson, to continue Atkinson's work.

The Duchess Garden, a parterre, at the north-west – or Nursery – end of Bowhill House, pictured in the spring of 1906. Originally a parterre was a flower garden laid out in a regular and ornamental manner and was a distinct art form in seventeenth-century France, being a feature of noble and royal residences. From this evolved the *parterres de broderie* (an embroidered parterre), using box hedging, coloured earth or gravel and turf, and later, once again, flowers. They became popular throughout Britain in the late nineteenth century. This fine example at Bowhill is probably the work of the garden designer William Sawry Gilpin (1762–1843), who is known to have worked on the estate's landscaping. It is noted in the 1986 Countryside Commission Survey, but disappeared in the early 1990s.

Under a celebration arch on the driveway at Bowhill, welcoming their arrival as newly weds, are Lady Constance Anne Scott (1877–1970), the youngest daughter of William Henry Walter Montague-Douglas-Scott, 6th Duke of Buccleuch, and her husband, the Honourable Douglas Halyburton Cairns (1867–1936), son of Hugh McCalmont Cairns, 1st Earl Cairns. They had married that morning – Tuesday, 21 January 1908 – in the chapel at Dalkeith Palace, the Duke of Buccleuch's Midlothian seat, and travelled to Bowhill for the first part of their honeymoon. There were no decorations at the estate's Yarrow road entrance, but this massive arch of evergreens, festooned with artificial roses, had been constructed on the avenue.

Foulshiels farmhouse and, in the foreground, the roadside cottage where the African explorer Mungo Park was born on 11 September 1771. Although Africa would ultimately take up much of his life's work, Dr Park graduated from Edinburgh University in 1791 and joined the Sumatra-bound ship *Worcester* the following year as assistant surgeon. Only in 1795, having been accepted by the African Association, did he become the first European in the Gambia, searching for the source of the River Niger. In 1799 he returned to Scotland, practicing as a surgeon in Peebles and marrying Alice Anderson at Kelso on 1 August that year. However, Africa was in his blood and in 1806 he returned to the Gambia where he drowned fighting off natives. On Foulshiels Hill, above the farm, runs the old drove road.

Newark Castle – originally 'New Werk' to distinguish it from an earlier 'Old Werk' castle – photographed from the Yarrow road beyond Foulshiels. Standing on a flat-topped knoll, within a barmkin, i.e. defensive wall, the 65 by 40 feet oblong tower-house first appears in surviving records of 1423. From 1432 to 1446 it was home to the Earls of Douglas and from 1470 was owned by Patrick de Moravia (Murray). It was besieged by English forces under Lord Gray of Wilton in 1547/48 but, although the barmkin was breached and the stables burned, the tower proved impregnable – until the following year. After the Battle of Philiphaugh on 13 September 1645, the Marquis of Montrose had 100 prisoners slaughtered in the courtyard. Its last military significance came in 1650 when it was used by Oliver Cromwell's army. Sometime in the eighteenth century the roof was removed and the valuable stone facings taken.

Broadmeadows Bridge, spanning the Yarrow Water, with Broadmeadows House on the hill above and the North Lodge gatehouse and entrance to Bowhill on the left.

Broadmeadows House in the summer of 1908. The plain Grecian-style house was built in 1853 by the Honourable William Napier, but by the 1890s it was being rented by Robert J. Lang, who had succeeded his father, H.M. Lang, as tenant.

The row of cottages at Yarrowford running to the west entry into Broadmeadows, pictured around 1911. The hamlet first appears on John Thomson's 1832 map of Scotland and developed to have a school and, later, a post office. The water pump in the foreground was stolen in the early 1990s.

Hangingshaw House in the summer of 1914. Standing in 8,500 acres, the original Hangingshaw Castle started as a tower house built by the Murrays of Fala in 1461, but was superseded by a house in the early eighteenth century. This house appears on General Roy's 1750 map but burnt down in 1766. James Murray had it rebuilt in 1769, but was forced to sell the following year. It was bought by a Mr Johnstone of Alva, thought to be John Johnstone (1734–1830) who, with the Honourable East India Company Service, commanded the artillery at the Battle of Plassey in 1757. The Johnstones built the house seen here in 1846 and, although they retained it until 1924, the 1901 census shows it occupied by 26-year-old John Croil Meek, a Walkerburn-born man of 'independent means'.

Captioned 'Miss Stewart – Yarrow – winding pirns' (i.e. winding yarn onto bobbins), this 1915 photograph shows 67-year-old Miss Margaret Stewart, who lived at Old Lewinshope Cottage with her brothers Robert, a general labourer, and Andrew, a woollen weaver. The cottage had been the family home of their parents, James Stewart (born 1802), a woollen weaver, and his wife Isabella (born 1817), and to which Margaret had later returned. She died at the cottage on 25 March 1916.

The ruin of the double-arch, rubble-built Old Bridge across the River Yarrow at Deuchar, some 70 yards downstream of the Deuchar Burn. The bridge had a span of 30 feet and carried a 12 feet and 6 inch-wide carriageway. A late seventeenth-century bridge, bearing the arms of the Duchess of Buccleuch (granted 1663), is recorded as being on the same site in 1722, but this was damaged by flood in 1734 and either rebuilt or replaced in 1748. It is not known whether the structure pictured is the 1734 ruin or the bridge of 1748.

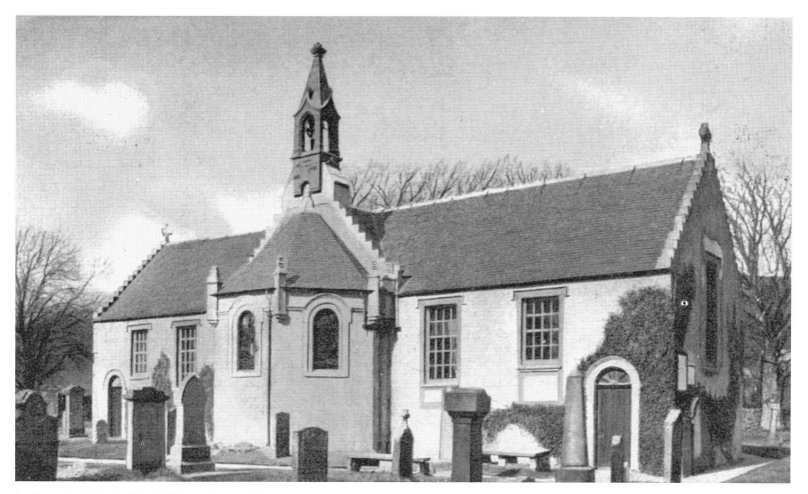

In the early 1640s the Rev. William Elliot and his congregation abandoned the thirteenth-century St Mary's of the Lowes Church (also known as St Mary's of the Forest) for the new, more centrally positioned, Yarrow Kirk. It was rebuilt in 1771 and underwent restoration work in 1826 and 1906, but was destroyed by fire in 1922 and rebuilt the following year. In the *New Statistical Account* (Yarrow Parish 1833), the Rev. Robert Russell (1766–1847) wrote that the 500 seats were divided among the heritors, according to their valuation, and by them among their tenants. Russell was succeeded by his son, also Robert (1809–1884), who penned *Reminiscences of Yarrow* (published in Edinburgh in 1886). At the time of this 1911 photograph the incumbent was the Rev. Robert Borland (1849–1912).

Photographed in the autumn of 1972, Harry Turnbull of Ladhope Farm (top right) feeds oat sheaves into a threshing machine, built by Clayton & Shuttleworth of Stamp End Works, Lincoln, which was driven by a Ford 30 tractor. He is assisted by his son Leslie (bottom), who is tending the outflow, and Lawrence Davidson, the mole catcher from Newark. The 30 acres of oats (producing one ton of grain per acre), cut with the reaper binder the previous week, had been standing drying in stooks. The farm has a long history, appearing in the Exchequer Rolls between 1455 and 1468 as a forest steading, paying £6 (Scots) and one bow cow per annum to the King.

When opened in 1907, through the generosity of Mr W. Strang Steel and the Duke of Buccleuch, Yarrow Hall – with its 160-seat hall, library, council room and caretaker's house – was hailed as another improvement in the valley, to stand alongside the founding of the agricultural show (1906) and the renovation of Yarrow Kirk the previous December. Sited on Catslackburn Haugh, near the then smithy, it was built of common rubble and finished in roughcast with freestone dressings and topped with olive-green Westmoreland slate. The main contractor was Messrs Ingles & Dickson of Selkirk, with joinery work by Messrs W. & T. Hobkirk of Hawick, slating and plumbing by Messrs John Tweedie & Son of Galashiels, and plasterwork by Clapperton & Son of Selkirk. By the roadside to the right is Oversby Cottage.

A 1918 view from Sundhope Hill, across the Yarrow Water to the Yarrow Feus United Free Church and its manse on the right, with the 'Plantation' at the Sundhope road end in the centre background. At the Disruption in 1843 over 400 ministers broke away from the Church of Scotland and founded new congregations under the banner of the Free Church of Scotland. This church, along with a manse for the Rev. Thomas McCrindle, was built in 1845 for a congregation of 107 worshippers from Yarrow and Meggat.

Yarrow Feus Post Office in 1903 with 36-year-old Adam Scott, who was both sub-post master and blacksmith, standing to the right with a pony. Adam was born in this house on 28 October 1866 and succeeded his father, also Adam, as blacksmith, and later took on the post office. He had, however, spent time in Aberdeenshire where he met and married Maggie Anderson, bringing along her sister Matilda, who acted as sub-post mistress for a time. The post office survived until about 1990. The name Yarrow Feus originated in the 1790s when land from Catslackburn Farm, along the north side of the road, was feued off. The Rev. Robert Russell wrote in the *New Statistical Account* that, 'A spirit of feuing at present prevails among the people. One whole farm belonging to the Duke of Buccleugh [*sic*] was this year feued out into small parcels, upon which the feuers are building very neat houses.'

The 'Plantation' roadside cottages at Yarrow Feus, where the road on the left turns down to Sundhope. Around 1920, when this photograph was taken, the two-storey house was occupied by labourer George Goodfellow, whose wife took care of ex-borstal and wayward boys. William Lyon, a tailor, lived with his family in the adjacent single-storey cottage.

Miss Jessie Allan in the garden of her one-room, clay-floored cottage by the bridge at Bengerburn (the cottage was later demolished, along with the bridge, although the road was then improved and the bridge rebuilt). She appears in the 1881 census as a 52-year-old, Inverness-born housekeeper to the shepherd Robert Melrose at Craig Douglas. In the census of 1901 she is listed as a native of Yarrow. Following her death on Friday, 12 March 1915, the *Southern Reporter* obituary noted that '. . . her strong individuality, her simple piety, and her many reminiscences of the olden times made her a great favourite with all the visitors who frequented the valley.'

The road and meandering Yarrow Water beyond Townhead, looking towards Catkerwood, Bengerburn and the Gordon Arms Hotel, around 1910. The heap of stones marks the site of one of the many small roadside quarries opened when the road was built and kept as a source for maintenance and repair.

Opposite: The Gordon Arms Hotel at Mountbenger on the Selkirk–Moffat road, photographed from the Tushielaw road which, across the junction, becomes the Paddy Slacks on its way to Innerleithen. The name Paddy Slacks derives either from the time when Mary, Queen of Scots, and her French-speaking retinue passed through and left the name *Pas des Lacs* ('Way to the Lakes'), or – more probably – from the adjacent Paddock stream and slacks, meaning 'boggy hollow'. The hotel is thought to date from the 1820s, when it may have initially been called the Mountbenger Inn. It was renamed Gordon after the builder or contractor who was employed in the construction of the Hartleap road. As it had no stables, it was not a staging post, nor did it hire horses, but nonetheless it was a favourite stopping place. It is said to have hosted the last meeting of Sir Walter Scott and James Hogg in 1830.

GORDON ARMS HOTEL,
❦ YARROW. ❦

An advertisement for the Gordon Arms Hotel from 1894 when attractions included free angling on the Yarrow Water and St Mary's Loch, a small golf course, and carriage and horse hire at moderate rates.

FREE ANGLING on the YARROW (which runs close to the Hotel), and in the smaller streams in the neighbourhood; also in ST MARY'S LOCH.

*

SMALL GOLF COURSE.
♦ ♦
CARRIAGES AND HORSES ON HIRE.
TERMS MODERATE.

*

The GORDON ARMS is 13 miles from Selkirk, and 9 from Innerleithen. From both places Coaches run every Tuesday, Thursday, and Saturday during summer months—3 miles from St Mary's Loch.

Telegraph within Two Miles.

WALTER BEATTIE.

Address—GORDON ARMS,
SELKIRK, N.B.

These Edwardian boating parties on St Mary's Loch would have been guests at Tibbie Shiel's Inn where three boats – for pleasure or fishing – were kept for visitors.

Two photographs of Tibbie Shiel at St Mary's Cottage, one by the Moffat photographer Thomas Hood, and the other – with her son William or 'Wullie' – taken by the Selkirk photographer A.R. Edwards a few years later. The daughter of Walter Shiel and Mary Grieve, Isobel, Isabella, or 'Tibbie', was born near Ettrick Kirk in 1783 and, in November 1806, married Robert Richardson, a Westmorland-born mole catcher, then working on Thirlestane Estate. In 1823 they moved from Chapelhope to St Mary's Cottage, a shooting lodge on Thirlestane Estate. Robert died the following March, leaving Tibbie with at least the younger of their six children to support. At that time her children were Thomas (1808–1890), Walter (born 1810), Margaret (born 1812), William (born 1816), Mary (born 1818) and Dorothy (born 1820). Their first daughter, Mary, baptized on 5 January 1810, had died in 1813. Thomas, Walter, and perhaps Margaret, would have left home for work, leaving their three younger siblings. It would not have been unusual for a roadside cottage to have offered hospitality to travellers (the same was happening further along the Moffat road at Birkhill) and soon St Mary's Cottage was on its way to becoming an inn.

Following Tibbie's death in July 1878, aged 96, William – by then in his early sixties – carried on the business, assisted by a nephew, Henry Burton, as ostler, and Helen Linton (born 1854), who was a granddaughter of Tibbie's sister Margaret. William died in November 1891 while on his way to Moffat for provisions, and sometime later Helen and her husband James Scott (born in Henderland in 1854) took over the business. In this photograph Helen sits with her parasol by the door, while James Scott can be seen in the window to the left. The group would have been guests.

As can be seen by the extensions and additions to the building, the years had moved on by the time this photograph was taken, but James Scott was still running the business and, following Helen's death, he married Agnes Kerr of Cardrona who is seated on the bench with the dog. The maid in the doorway is thought to be Kitty Davidson. When James died in 1922, his son Adam and his wife Christine were hosts until 1949 when the business was sold. The horse in the photograph is thought to have been called Polly.

This photograph was captioned 'Clock at Tibbie's, St Mary's Loch', implying a closer connection with Tibbie herself than was the case. The 6-feet high, three-hundredweight clock case was carved from elm from Craigieburn Wood – a favourite haunt of the poet Robert Burns around 1789, and the birthplace of Jean Lorimer, his 'Chloris' – by one John Wilson, who may have been the Moffat-born (in 1817) journeyman mason who lived at West Burnside. Standing on castors, the clock had a short pendulum and a cylindrical musical box mechanism with twelve 'Scottish Tunes'. It was seen, dusty and neglected, in Scott the builder's premises in Moffat by Christine Scott, possibly at the time of some of the extensions and improvements, and bought for the inn. When the inn was sold in 1949 it was gifted to Dumfries Museum, but was found to be so riddled with woodworm it was thought advisable to have it exported to America.

An advertisement for tours of the Ettrick and Yarrow valleys from William Angus's book, *Ettrick and Yarrow – A Guide* (1894).

A convoy of carriages making its way along the Captain's Road from Crosscleuch, by the Devil's Elbow, and heading towards Berrybush from where they may have turned for either the Gordon Arms on the Yarrow or the Tushielaw Inn on the Ettrick.

The view of St Mary's Loch from the Devil's Elbow.

In the mountain pass on the Selkirkshire–Dumfriesshire boundary, Birkhill was a shepherd's cottage and from around 1820, when it was the home of James Hastie and his wife Jean Aitchison, an 'open house' to travellers. Around 1843 John Broadfoot, a native of Crawford in Lanarkshire, came to Birkhill from Laverhay in Wamphray with his wife Janet (or Jenny) Rogerson of Moffat, and at least three children – Helen (born 1830), William (born 1831) and Isabella (born 1939). Jenny became 'mine host' and as well known for her hospitality as Tibbie over at St Mary's as, by that time, the wild scenery around Loch Skeen and the Grey Mare's Tail were becoming popular tourist haunts. John died in 1867 at the age of 64 and Jenny in 1876 at 73, leaving their daughter Helen, or Ailie, who had married James Wightman in 1852, to run the house and the business. In the 1680s this remote, mountainous, moorland was a haunt of Covenanters; Watch Hill, to the west of Birkhill, was a station for their watchman. Four of the Covenanters were shot near the inn doorway by order of John Graham of Claverhouse, who was later killed at the Battle of Killiecrankie in 1689.

A poster, printed by John Lewis of Selkirk, advertising the Yarrow & Ettrick Pastoral Society's Great Annual Show of 1909, held at the Gordon Arms on Saturday, 18 September. Founded in 1906 and still going strong – with the object of improving breeds of sheep (particularly cheviot and blackface), cattle, horses (encouraging the breeding and training of hunters suitable to the Borders), and the domestic practices of baking, butter-making and cookery – the society embraced the parishes of Yarrow, Ettrick, Kirkhope, Ashkirk and Selkirk.

The president and committee of the Yarrow & Ettrick Pastoral Society of 1972. *Back row* (left to right): Robert Jackson, Philiphaugh; Harry Turnbull, Ladhope; John Plenderleith, Riskenhope; Robert Anderson, Shiringscleuch; Jack Davidson, East Deloraine; President James Wilson, Hutlerburn; James Mitchell, Henderland; William Thompson, Muchra; Fred Anderson, Philiphaugh; Lachie Hamilton, Oakwood Mill; Sam McClymont, Tinnis; Harry Scott, Cacrabank; Walter Barrie, Eldinhope; and the secretary, Hamish Brown. *Front row*: Peter Scott, Selkirk; Robert McFadzean, Scabcleuch; Walter Hume, Sundhope; Tom Hogg, Headshaw; and Billy Amos, Synton Mains.

The suspension bridge over the Ettrick Water at Brockhill in the early 1900s. According to local knowledge, it may have been moved from Ettrickshaws in the early 1890s as a similar construction there was replaced by an iron bridge in 1891 (see page 42), and this seems to be borne out by William Angus who recorded in his 1894 book that, '. . . a footbridge recently thrown across the stream forms a convenient way for getting to Brockhill'. The ford to the left of the footbridge would have been the river crossing before the building of the Ettrick Bridge in 1628. This bridge was lost in a spate in October 1977 and replaced.

Passing through the gorge under Ettrick Bridge, the river ran to the cauld that in part diverted it into the lade serving Howfordmill, the building on the right in this 1920 photograph. The mill has long been out of service and the lade partially infilled.

A view of the village of Ettrickbridge, running north west from the bridge. In 1628 Sir Walter 'Wat' Scott of Harden spanned the gorge with a three-arch bridge that, due to a design fault, was a ruin by 1715. The present bridge, with later modifications, was built in 1780. According to legend, he built the bridge as a penance for the drowning of a young hostage he was bringing back from a raid. As the road straightens off the bridge, the church lich gate stands at the end of the wall on the right.

The 300-seat Kirkhope Parish Church in Woodend Road, photographed here in the summer of 1913, was built in 1839 by the 5th Duke of Buccleuch, Walter Francis Montagu-Douglas-Scott (1806–1884), for the convenience of parishioners in the outlying parts of both Yarrow and Ettrick. On 25 June 1851 the area around was disjoined from Yarrow and the parish of Kirkhope established, with John Sharpe Gibson (1816–1872) as its first minister. His mother, Jane Sharpe, was a great-granddaughter of Thomas Boston. Although there was already a school for 100 children, the Duke also endowed the village with another with accommodation for thirty pupils.

Ettrickbridge in the summer of 1912 with, on the left, the thatched post office, or 'Post Office Receiving House' as it was known when established by George Hope in 1859.

A late 1920s view of Ettrickbridge, with Mitchell the carpenter's premises on the right. Born at Lilliesleaf in 1800, Thomas Mitchell was in Yarrow by 1830, when he married Margaret Bryden. He may also have served his carpentry apprenticeship there. In the early 1860s he came to Ettrickbridge, where the business employed two men and two apprentices. No one in this photograph has, as yet, been identified, but the man in the carpenter's apron may be Mitchell's son, James, who was born in December 1844. Adjacent is the Cross Keys Inn.

The panorama across the village from the glebe to Brockhill Wood, pictured in 1907. Over the roof of Cherryden, in the foreground, can be picked out the Cross Keys and the school and the church in Woodend Road. The field with the hayricks would later become the football pitch.

Work started on the building of Ettrick Shaws House and stables soon after Dr Thomas Scott Anderson MD, JP, MFH (Master of Foxhounds) (1853–1919) completed the purchase of 30 acres of land from Buccleuch Estate on 14 July 1891. The son of Dr Thomas Anderson of Selkirk, he was educated at Edinburgh's Merchiston School and graduated as MD from the *Ecole de Medecine* in Paris. He emigrated to Australia where, in 1876, he married Joan A. Shaw of Wooriwyrite, Victoria. Perhaps, because Joan's father, Thomas Shaw, was founder of the Victorian Stud Merino Sheep Breeders Association, he took an interest in sheep. They had returned from Australia shortly before purchasing the Buccleuch land. A wooden suspension bridge was taken down – and perhaps resited at Brockhill – and this iron bridge, bearing on either side 'P & W MacLellan of the Clutha Ironworks, Glasgow, 1891', replaced it. Founded in 1811, MacLellan's had opened their new Clutha works in the city's Kinning Park area in 1871 and remained major producers and exports of ironwork until their closure in 1979. In the late 1940s the house opened as Ettrickshaws Country House Hotel.

A view of Ettrick Shaws House and the stable block beyond from the summer of 1910.

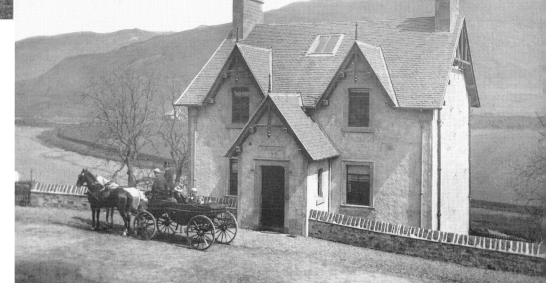

An Edwardian family outing, possibly from Selkirk, stops at the Tushielaw Inn. The name Tushielaw, or Torchelaw, first appeared in 1455 when the Crown seized Torchelaw Tower and its lands from the Douglas family. It became home to the Scotts until Adam Scott, 'King of Thieves' or 'King of the Border', fell foul of King James V who had him beheaded at Edinburgh on 27 July 1529. In 1688 it was bought by a Michael Anderson. The inn does not appear on John Thomson's 1832 *Atlas of Scotland*, but compiling his account of the Parish of Yarrow in September 1833, for the *New Statistical Account*, the Rev. James Smith recorded that, 'Two years ago [1831] a new inn was built on the banks of the Ettrick, near the old mansion of Tushielaw. It is neatly fitted up and has several comfortable apartments.' Although it was not a coaching inn – there was no stagecoach service on this route – it served as a toll house on the lucrative cattle route between Hawick and Peebles.

The Tushielaw Inn, photographed from the right bank of the Ettrick Water a summer or two before the previous illustration, when it was run by Midlothian-born Peter Smith and was also home to him and his wife Margaret and their four children. The Ettrick is thought a good trout river – by fly or worm – and in the spawning season is said to be full of salmon and sea trout.

The rear of Thirlestane House, photographed around 1909. Built in the early nineteenth century, from stone taken from an earlier house, it was ready for plasterwork in 1813, although over the entrance was a panel bearing the inscription, 'WN ECJ 1820' – a reference to Captain William John, 9th Lord Napier of Merchiston (1786–1834), and his wife Eliza Cochrane-Johnstone (c.1795–1883), whom he married in 1816. Having succumbed to dry rot, the house was demolished in the 1960s.

Following the opening of the Scottish Youth Hostel Association's first hostel at Broadmeadows earlier in the year, the Factor's House at Thirlestane was put at the association's disposal by Lord Napier on very generous terms and opened on Saturday, 20 June 1931. With accommodation for 30 hikers (fifteen of each sex), the press described the house as being, '. . . situated in a charming position, near the highway, encircled by trees and with the river nearby.' It remained popular until shortly before its closure in October 1950. Built as a mill in 1687, part of the lade survives and a barn was added in 1867. Although recorded in the 1881 census as the 'Factor's House', it was occupied at that time by James Gray, coachman, and his wife, Isabella, and would have been the stables and coach-house. The building was falling into decrepitude by the turn of the twentieth century, and this photograph was taken before the association's acquisition. Today, as a private house, the ivy is gone and the building gleams in a beige snowcem coat.

Ramsaycleuch farmhouse, pictured in 1929. Built above the road in 1874, it replaced the original three-storey roadside farmhouse, which was then demolished. Alexander Scott (born 1831) was the tenant of the 1,700 acre farm on Thirlestane Estate. On the day details were taken for the 1881 census the farmhouse was occupied by Scott, along with his 43-year-old Hawick-born wife, Helen, and their six children – John (aged 18), Jeannie (12), Minnie (10), Christina (9), Helen (7), and Henry (4). Staff included John Crozier (25), shepherd; Jane Jardaine (24), cook; Margaret Brown, their 23-year-old housekeeper; and there were three 'vagrants' – George Deans (42) of Peebles; Thomas Armstrong (41) of Annan; and Andrew Salton (26) of Lasswade. By 1917 it was occupied by William Thomson from Horsleyhill near Ancrum, and his family still run it today.

Ettrick Post Office, pictured around 1912. Selkirk Post Office opened in July 1768, but at Ettrick, as in Yarrow, records of early post offices are, at best, poor. In 1852 a 'post office receiving house' opened within the grocer's shop at Ramsaycleuch, which by 1867 – when owned by James Amos (born 9 January 1816) – was receiving mail from Selkirk on Tuesdays, Thursdays and Saturdays and dispatching it on Mondays, Wednesdays and Fridays. The sparse records show that in 1884, when Amos would have been 68 years old and on the point of retiring, Ramsaycleuch Post Office closed and Ettrick Post Office opened. Sometime after this photograph was taken an anonymous postbox (i.e. without royal cipher) was installed on the gable wall. The post office closed on 28 July 2004.

The road to Ettrick Kirk – with the Boston Memorial Hall on the left and, opposite, Ettrick Public School and the schoolmaster's house – photographed in the summer of 1924. Named in memory of the 'fire and brimstone' preacher, the Rev. Thomas Boston (1676–1732), the hall was opened in July 1909 by Miss Rose Haldane of Ettrick Hall, 'Lady Bountiful of Ettrick', who had donated not only the ground, but also the railings and most of the furnishings. Had Lord Napier's efforts (and his gift of £180) in the 1890s come to fruition there would have been a 'Jubilee Hall' in 1897, but there was a lack of interest and further funds. In 1906 efforts were again started to build a community hall, this time to commemorate the bi-centenary of Thomas Boston's appointment to Ettrick Church in 1707. It cannot be ascertained how much money was raised but, in addition to the land gifted by Miss Haldane, Mr Strang Steel of Philiphaugh gave £50, and Andrew Carnegie – the Dunfermline-born American industrialist and philanthropist – gifted £150 on learning that the hall would have a library. The opening day was a great success, including the speeches, and the teas and refreshments served by the Galashiels branch of the British Women's Temperance Association were followed by a concert which ended the day. Renovated in 1947 at a cost of £900, the hall still serves the community.

Ettrick Public School and the 'school cottage', photographed from the roadway around 1911. The 1863 Ordnance Survey map is unclear, but the cottage appears to have been the original school and schoolmaster's house. By 1911 the master lived in a new house behind the school, whilst the original building for a time housed those on parish relief. It was demolished in the late 1930s or forties and its last occupants were the sisters Martha (who rode a motorcycle to her work in the Rodona Hotel) and Christina Davidson. None of the nine girls or six boys can be named, but the teacher, to the left, may have been Andrew McLaren, with his wife Mary (wearing the hat) standing among the girls. Demolition of the school building started on 4 June 1964 and, with the site cleared, work started on the present school, which opened on 31 August 1965.